An Illustrated Hi

NORTON

THE IRON ROAD

by

Carol Fox

for
Garrin and Dillon
and the next generation

Front cover illustration by Mike Burton © copyright

Published by Fearns & Co., September 2000
Printed by Billingham Press

ISBN 1 903678 00 5

CONTENTS

INTRODUCTION ---------- 3
WHY BUILD A RAILROAD? ---------- 3
CANAL OR RAILROAD ---------- 4
THE PROPOSED CANAL ---------- 4
THE CANAL PLAN IS DOOMED ---------- 5
THE PROPOSED RAILROAD ---------- 7
EARLY RAILROADS ---------- 7
RAILWAY COMPANY TRIUMPHS ---------- 8
STOCKTON AND DARLINGTON RAILWAY COMMENCES ---------- 8
THE CLARENCE RAILWAY COMPANY ---------- 10
THE COMPANY'S BEGINNINGS ---------- 10
COMMITTEE MEMBERS ---------- 12
THE ROUTE OF THE CLARENCE RAILWAY ---------- 13
INTRODUCTION OF LOCOMOTIVE POWER ---------- 15
THE CLARENCE RAILWAY IN NORTON---------- 16
THE CONSTRUCTION OF NORTON JUNCTION ---------- 17
THE END OF THE CLARENCE RAILWAY COMPANY---------- 18
RALPH WARD JACKSON OF HARTLEPOOL ---------- 19
MESSRS FOSSICK AND HACKWORTH---------- 20
STEAM ENGINE BUILDING MANUFACTORY---------- 21
NORTH SHORE AND SH&C STATIONS---------- 22
FUSSICK BRIDGE---------- 23
EARLY RAIL TRAVEL---------- 24
HORSE-DRAWN TRAVEL---------- 24
LOCOMOTIVE TRAVEL---------- 24
A COMMUTER'S TALE---------- 25
RAILWAY WORKERS---------- 25
"RAILWAY MANIA"---------- 26
CRYSTAL PALACE EXHIBITION IN 1851---------- 27
NORTON JUNCTION---------- 28
EARLY BUILDINGS---------- 29
RESIDENTS AT NORTON JUNCTION---------- 30
THE INSPECTOR'S HOUSE---------- 32
EXCURSIONS AND HOLIDAYS---------- 33
ROYALTY AT NORTON JUNCTION---------- 35
NORTON STATION---------- 37
THE "HALT"---------- 37
THE STATION INN---------- 38
FROM STEAM TO DIESEL---------- 39
NORTON JUNCTION (DEVELOPMENT OF RAILWAY OPERATIONS)---------- 39
RAILWAY OPERATIONS FROM 1960---------- 41
EAST CURVE---------- 43
WEST CURVE ---------- 44
THE "BACK LINE" ---------- 45
DECLINE OF THE JUNCTION---------- 46
AFTER THE DECLINE---------- 48
A FARMER'S LAMENT---------- 50
CHRONOLOGY- THE CLARENCE AND ASSOCIATED RAILWAYS---------- 51

INTRODUCTION

Much has been written about the Stockton and Darlington railway, however it is less well known that the line running through Norton Junction belonged to the Clarence Railway and not the S&DR.

This book looks at the Clarence Railway and its significance in Norton's history.

WHY BUILD A RAILROAD?

The prime motive for setting up a railway system in north-east England in the early part of the 19th Century was to facilitate the speedier transportation of bulk items, especially coal from the collieries, to the nearest canal or river for despatch to London and other parts of the country, via the local ports.

In mediaeval England, Newcastle had established itself as the main centre for the coal industry. However, with the industrial revolution of the 18th Century, demand far exceeded supply. Many new coalfields were being opened up in the counties of Durham and Northumberland, and the only way at this time to transport the coal was by packs of overworked horses pulling heavy carts and wagons. One obvious method of speeding up the journey was to find a way to ease the loads on the animals – for instance by fitting the wagon wheels on to fixed rails.

The mining companies operating in Durham and Northumberland were fortunate in that the 3 rivers of Tyne, Tees and Wear allowed sufficient provision for the delivery of their coal. For them, alternative means of transport were deemed unnecessary. It was the rich unworked seams around the more outlying areas of the counties that prompted interest in direct colliery-to-port delivery, and at the beginning of the 19th Century two methods were presented as being viable – a canal or a railroad.

CANAL OR RAILROAD

The Proposed Canal

In other parts of the country bulk loads (grains, hides, lead etc.) were moved by a canal system that had proved both popular and fairly cheap to construct (mainly due to the cheap Irish labourers who worked in their hundreds – rough, tough, but hardworking and nicknamed "navvies"). Canals were man-made navigational channels (thus the name "navvies") which connected up, as far as possible, with existing rivers, thereby making use of available natural waterways, helping further to keep down some of the construction costs.

During the 18th Century so much "canalisation" had taken place that by 1810 some 2,000 miles of canals were in existence (though none in Durham and Northumberland where the new collieries were being opened up). At this time in its development the men of vision in Stockton felt that their town should reap some profit from these new coalfields, and methods of benefitting the port came under discussion. The new mines needed efficient transport and a canal would just fit the bill. At this time Yarm was of considerable importance as a port for the predominantly agricultural industries of the pre-railway north-eastern regions.

A canal for this area was by no means a new idea, for in 1768 a survey for a canal 27$^1/_2$ miles long running from Winston in County Durham to Stockton had been carried out by Mr James Brindley and Mr Robert Whitworth. The estimate of £63,000 was considered prohibitive and the plans were shelved – until four decades later.

In September 1810 a successful "cut" had been made in the River Tees at Stockton to help straighten the tortuously winding river and to shorten the shipping time from the port to the sea. During a meeting held in Stockton to mark the occasion, a far-reaching proposal was made which would affect not only the fortunes of Stockton but ultimately the world. Mr Leonard Raisbeck of Stockton moved a resolution, seconded by Mr Benjamin Flounders of Yarm, that a committee be set up to look into linking Stockton and the collieries, now that the port of Stockton was more accessible.

Mr Raisbeck, a solicitor and Stockton's Recorder, aware more than ever of the increasing need for a link between the Durham collieries and Stockton, called for a meeting with gentry and tradesmen to discuss the practicability of either a canal or a railway system. This meeting took place at the King's Head Hotel in Darlington in January 1812. Engineer Mr James Rennie was appointed to carry out the necessary survey. His report published in 1813 estimated that a canal from Stockton to Winston via Darlington, using the same route as that of Mr Robert Whitworth in 1768, would cost £95,600. As before, financial difficulties forced the cessation of plans.

Christopher Tennant (a native of Yarm but residing in Stockton) declared himself to be unhappy at laying the plans aside. He strongly advocated a canal rather than a railway, and to prove his convictions he commissioned yet another survey. Not only was this carried out at his own expense, but he also personally assisted Civil Engineer Mr George Leather in surveying a slightly different route. His estimate was in excess of £200,000.

The Canal Plan Is Doomed

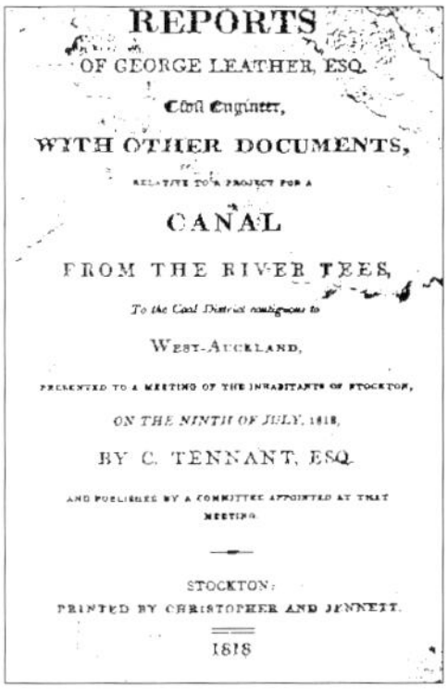
REPORTS
OF GEORGE LEATHER, ESQ.
Civil Engineer,
WITH OTHER DOCUMENTS,
RELATIVE TO A PROJECT FOR A
CANAL
FROM THE RIVER TEES,
To the Coal District contiguous to
WEST-AUCKLAND,
PRESENTED TO A MEETING OF THE INHABITANTS OF STOCKTON,
ON THE NINTH OF JULY, 1818,
BY C. TENNANT, ESQ.
AND PUBLISHED BY A COMMITTEE APPOINTED AT THAT MEETING.
STOCKTON:
PRINTED BY CHRISTOPHER AND JENNETT.
1818

The "canal versus railway" debate continued apace, with each of the two factions determined to be victor. Christopher Tennant pressed on with his plans for the "Stockton and Auckland Canal" and in July 1818 application was made for an Act of Parliament and for the collection of subscriptions.

The news of a revolutionary new way to transport not only coal from the coalfields but also other bulk loads, and eventually passengers, created some excitement and interest among the population in Norton. The local carriers were kept busy with a great number of visitors to the area – surveyors and engineers, land-owners and businessmen – although there wasn't much to see, other than great mounds of earth and coloured posts along the survey route.

The talk in the local alehouses and hostelries, however, was that the water millers were unhappy their water supply would cease unless another beck (though expensive) was dug alongside the proposed canal, as their present supply would be dammed in order to facilitate operation of the 44 proposed locks in the system. This resulted in their declaration not to sell their ancient land rights to the canal company. The dilemma was resolved with Mr Leather, the surveyor, proposing a clause that all water flow adjustments would be at the company's expense and any loss of revenue due to canal operations would be covered by an Act of Parliament when the scheme went for approval.

The proposed scheme forecast handsome dividends after the first five years and a number of local gentry subscribed. Among them were the Vicar (Rev. Christopher Anstey), 8 of Norton's land-owners and 2 of the millers, Mr Lax of Wolviston Mill and Mr Coates of Norton Mill.

Christopher Tennant had reckoned, though, without the intervention of those notables whose businesses would suffer badly if his scheme went ahead, for neither Yarm nor Darlington would be directly served by his canal. Dissenting voices were heard, among them Mr Jonathon Backhouse and the influential and wealthy Mr Edward Pease, Quaker gentlemen and merchants of Darlington (referred to as the "Darlington faction").

In October 1818, on completion of George Leather's survey, an Act of Parliament was sought to give assent for The Stockton and Auckland Canal. However, the £225,000 finance for this venture could not be found either, and it was with a heavy heart that the £35,000 raised locally was returned and the plans for a canal were finally laid to rest.

In November 1818, following Christopher Tennant's bitter disappointment over his canal, and before all hope of wealth from the Durham coalfields had dissipated, a committee was appointed to look into the practicability of that other method previously suggested – a railroad – which could shorten still further the distance to the collieries and yet include the town of Darlington. This way none of the local millers would lose their livelihoods, and besides a railroad should enable goods to be moved many times faster than a canal route for possibly less outlay. Mr Leonard Raisbeck and Col. Sleigh of Norton addressed the meeting held in Stockton Town Hall.

The death knell of the "Stockton and Auckland Canal" had been sounded, but this was not the last we have heard of entrepreneur Christopher Tennant.

Mr Edward Pease

The Proposed Railroad

Meanwhile, Mr Raisbeck, still resolute about a communication link with the collieries, had suggested a survey be carried out by Welsh engineer Mr George Overton (a relative of Mr Jeremiah Cairns of Yarm) into the feasibility of a railroad over that of a canal. Mr Overton was fully qualified to carry this out, having laid down some 70 miles of small railways in South Wales. This proved to be the preferred choice, and Mr Overton's findings in favour of a railway, costing £124,000, were accepted. It looked as though the Stockton and Darlington Railway Company would triumph after all.

On 13th November 1818 the resolution was passed to apply for an Act of Parliament – it was rejected. Mr Overton's proposals were said to be flawed. Mr Edward Pease, an influential wool merchant and banker from Darlington, a prime promoter of the railway, declared himself to be unhappy with the route, and engineer Mr George Stephenson was asked to conduct a further survey for a railroad from Stockton via Darlington to the coalfields.

Early railroads

The earliest documented iron railroad had been laid as far back as 1760 in Colebrookdale (where the first ever iron bridge in the world was erected and is today a popular tourist attraction) and a variety of steam engines had been experimented with on private railroads by the early part of the 19th century. Much has been written by railway experts on these early railroads and engines, but we are looking here at public locomotive railways and their beginnings.

Railway Company Triumphant as First Railway Bill is Passed

A promoters' meeting was held in the George and Dragon Hotel, High Street, Yarm on 12th February 1820 at which Thomas Meynell of Yarm presided. George Overton assisted by David Davies examined the route yet again and submitted their new report in 1820.

A renewed application was made for Parliamentary powers and on 19th April 1821 the first Railway Bill was passed for a line carrying raw materials from Witton Park in County Durham to Stockton in County Durham, with 5 branches.

Stockton and Darlington Railway Commences

In May that year (1821) Thomas Meynell was elected Chairman of the Stockton and Darlington Railway Company (S&DR). The first sod of earth was cut in September that year at St. John's Well, Bridge Road, Stockton-on-Tees by Mr George Stephenson. George Stephenson was appointed Engineer on 22 January 1822 with a salary of £600 per annum. The first rail was laid on 23 May 1822 by Thomas Meynell, and the Stockton and Darlington Railway (S&DR) Company was in business.

The S&DR seal which translates as "At Private Risk for Public Service"

However, one more amendment was necessary before the railways we know today became popular. The Railway Bill had been passed to develop the use of railroads for transporting coals and heavy goods – but not for the use of steam or locomotive engines on these rails (the wagons were still horse-drawn). This was empowered by the second Railway Act in May

1823 and from this point in time George Stephenson is synonymously linked with railways and trains.

Mr George Stephenson

The solicitors for the S&DR were Leonard Raisbeck of Stockton (he of the initial suggestion of a colliery link back in 1810) and Francis Mewburn of Darlington. The treasurers were Jonathon Backhouse Jnr. of Darlington (until 1833) then Joseph Pease of Darlington (both Quaker gentlemen). The Chairman (from 1821-1828) was Thomas Meynell. The Engineers were George Overton and David Davies in 1820, George Stephenson of Wylam in 1821, Timothy Hackworth of Wylam in 1825, and Thomas Storey from 1825.

Mr Timothy Hackworth

On 27th September 1825 the S&DR ran its very first train. A procession set off from Brusselton near Shildon in County Durham headed by George Stephenson's ***"Locomotion"*** No.1 pulling the coach "***Experiment***" and 38 assorted coach wagons overflowing with passengers.

Locomotion No.1

Although the company went from strength to strength there were internal disputes, and in May 1828 Thomas Meynell and Leonard Raisbeck resigned their posts, due in part to plans for extending the line southwards towards the new town of Middlesbrough (to Stockton's possible detriment) rather than northwards. The influential Edward Pease went on to found the new port of Middlesbrough (also known as Port Darlington).

THE CLARENCE RAILWAY COMPANY

The Company's Beginnings

Mr Christopher Tennant

The S&DR was undoubtedly a success, but there was still room for a railway serving a different route. On 19th January 1828 Christopher Tennant's name resurfaced with a letter in "The Durham County Advertiser" outlining his plans for another railroad to the collieries – this to be designated The Clarence Railway. In this letter he outlined his disappointment at the defeat of his "Stockton and Auckland Canal" and furnished information regarding his personal involvement with subsequent surveys of his proposed route, along with his hopes and desires for a new railroad. He made mention also of his proposal in 1824 to form the Tees and Weardale Railway, a name now no longer appropriate to the route ascribed to his new project. His subsequent letter in the "Durham County Advertiser" of 27th August 1830 applauded the perseverance of the Committee and promoters of The Clarence Railway and ended with the words "... victory is the reward".

This railroad was to be 6 miles shorter than the S&DR by virtue of the fact that it served neither Darlington nor Yarm, its terminus being at Haverton Hill (Samphire Batts), nearer to the mouth of the River Tees.

On the 23rd May 1828 Royal Assent was given to an Act to allow the Clarence Railway line to run from Haverton Hill to Sim Pasture Farm (near Heighington in County Durham), where it would connect up with the S&DR line. Further Acts in 1829 and 1833 allowed alterations to the branch lines and extensions from Haverton Hill to Samphire Batts (Port Clarence) and from Samphire Batts to Saltholme. On 21st June 1828 Christopher Tennant was the special guest of honour at a public dinner in honour of the Clarence Railway Company, and Mr Henry Blanshard was acknowledged for his unstinting perseverance in help to bring Christopher Tennant's plans to fruition.

A poem was published by Mr Thomas Webber, the poet laureate of Stockton, entitled " *Lines on the Clarence Railway and the intended Improvement of the River Tees*", in honour of Mr Tennant. It goes like this:

> *"Sons of the Tees! Whose deeds for ages past*
> *Were seldom equalled – never were surpassed –*
> *Whose ANNALS boast of many a worthy name,*
> *Rendered immortal by the trump of Fame –*
> *By their departed shades, now hovering near,*
> *By all you hope for, reverence, and revere,*
> *Tread in their footsteps, emulate your sires,*
> *Till the last spark of life's dull lamp expires;*
> *Unite with* TENNANT *in the Railway cause,*
> *Improve the Tees, and gain the world's applause;*
> *So will your Commerce and your Trade increase,*
> *With all the blessings of domestic Peace."*

Christopher Tennant's early years as a sailor in the British Navy and his high regard for the then Lord Admiral of the British Navy, the Duke of Clarence, (later King William IV), had led him to designate the line the "Clarence Railway". The motto *"Perseverando"* is particularly apt. He was naturally of a scientific mind and a fluent speaker, a man of such winning personality that he was able to turn men to his cause through sheer hard work and ability.

The seal of the Clarence Railway Company

Committee Members

The first General Meeting was held on the 3rd July 1828 to elect a working committee to run the Company. Mr John Page of Norton (a farmer and a tanner, and later a JP, of Red House, overlooking Norton Green) was elected to the committee.

The treasurer was Mr William Skinner, Jnr., the clerk/secretary was Mr John Smith, and the Chairman was Henry Vansittart Esq. Mr Edward Steel (at one time George Stephenson's assistant) was the first engineer until October 1833, then Mr Thomas King until November 1834, followed by Mr Thomas Rhodes. Sir William Foulis, Bart. was a Director and the Deputy Chairman. The other Directors included Mr Henry Blanshard, Mr John Holt Skinner, Mr Thomas Richmond, Mr John Russell Rowntree, Mr Thomas Allison Tennant, Mr R Appleby, Mr Richard Dixon, Mr J Stagg, Mr T Simpson and the Rev H Hildyard. Later were added Mr W Morrice (London), Mr B J Salvin (Croxdale Hall), Mr J Addie, M.D., Mr J Page, Mr T Walker and Mr S Walton.

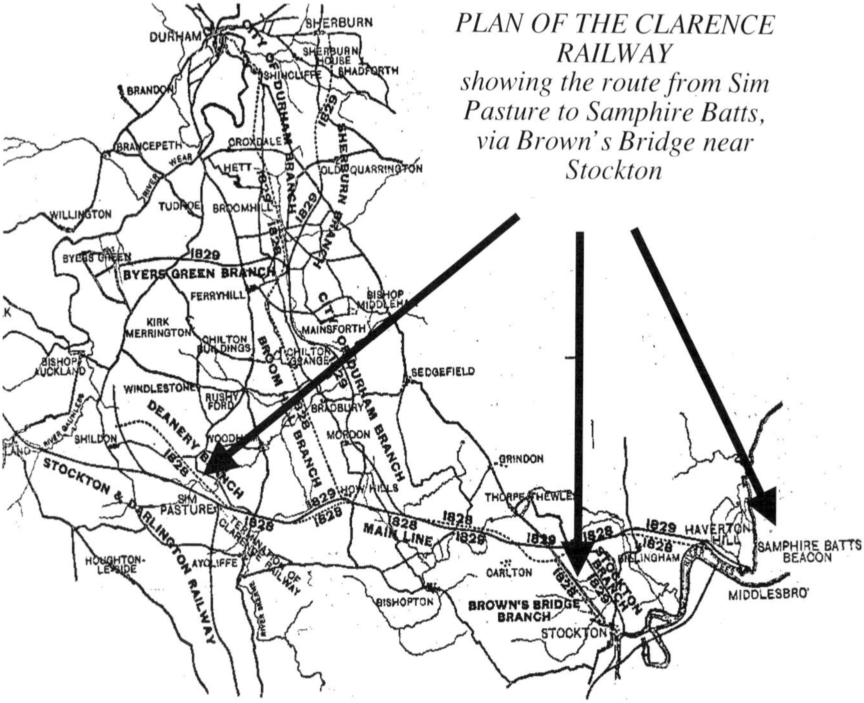

PLAN OF THE CLARENCE RAILWAY showing the route from Sim Pasture to Samphire Batts, via Brown's Bridge near Stockton

The Route of the Clarence Railway

The line was to run from Haverton Hill to Sim Pasture Farm in County Durham, a total of 14 miles, with a branch from Harrogate House at the eastern side of the Yarm turnpike road between Norton and Blakeston via Brown's Bridge to the Tees at Stockton. (This branch was altered to its present position by an Act in 1829.)

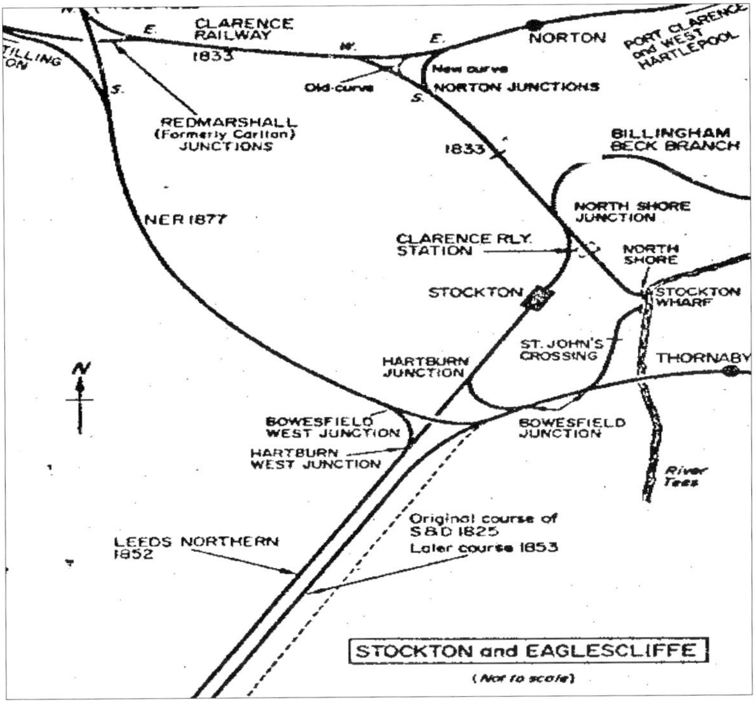

Sim Pasture to Stockton by S&DR was 17½ miles, by the Clarence Railway 11½ miles. A saving of 6 miles. Sim Pasture to the shipping port at Middlesbrough by the S&DR would be 21½ miles, but to the port of Haverton Hill by the Clarence Railway 14 miles. A saving of 7½ miles. Because it was a direct line from the collieries to the shipping port (which, being nearer the Tees mouth, boasted deeper staithes even at low tides) and it avoided Darlington and Yarm, the saving was 7½ miles, one-third of the distance, on the S&DR line. The gauge was to be the same as the S&DR (4'8½").

The coal "drops" at Port Clarence built in 1834 by the Clarence Railway Company, connected by a rail system to the Durham collieries. In 1839 over a quarter of a million tons of coal were shipped from these staithes

Construction of the line began in 1829 and by August 1833 coals were being delivered to Stockton via the Stockton and Clarence branch lines. On 29th October the Clarence's own staithes were in use at Stockton quayside, followed on 30th January 1834 by a small staith at Haverton Hill and then a few months later a deep water staith at Samphire Batts (Port Clarence), the "drops" to George Leather's suggestion.

Coal staithes at Seaham Harbour

INTRODUCTION OF LOCOMOTIVE POWER

Locomotive engines began to supersede horsepower on the S&DR lines in September 1833, while the Clarence lines introduced steam on some lines two years later. Locomotives were not used exclusively, for in 1836 both steam and horse-drawn engines were used on the main line from Sim Pasture to Port Clarence. An interesting feature of the Clarence system was that their trains ran on the right instead of the left-hand side of the road. Only one other company, the Newcastle and Carlisle Railway Company, also flouted the established custom in this respect.

The Clarence was one of the three companies in the North of England to use locomotive engines built to a design different to that of the Stephensons in 1830. Most of the company's engines were of similar construction to those used on the S&DR lines, though at least one of the alternative engines had been built by Hackworth and Downing of Shildon.

The passenger traffic (handled by a private lessee) was hauled by the *"Victory"* (built by William Lister of Darlington) and the *"Norton"* (built by R & W Hawthorn). Other Clarence engines included the *"Seymour"*, the *"Pilot"* and the *"Sir Robert Peel"* (pre-1837). The established engine companies (Stephensons, Hackworth, Hawthorn, Kitching) all supplied engines to several different companies, the keen competition resulting in much experimentation and the introduction of more reliable engines.

Engine No.60051 passing Roseworth and the south signal box

THE CLARENCE RAILWAY IN NORTON

A typical scene during the 1840s as a locomotive-driven train pulling two composite coaches steams into Norton Junction

The line currently in use at Norton Junction and the west curve was built as part of the Clarence Railway system in 1832 and formed part of the Stockton Branch, which ran for a distance of just over 2 miles to the port of Stockton on the River Tees.

The Clarence Railway Company had been incorporated in July 1828 under Christopher Tennant to transport coal from the West Durham collieries to the ports of Stockton and Port Clarence. The system consisted of a main line from Port Clarence to the S&DR junction at Sim Pasture running for 15 miles, 4 furlongs and 2 chains. There were five branches as follows:

City of Durham Branch	13 miles 0 furlongs 0 chains
Sherburn Branch	5 miles 6 furlongs 3 chains
Byers Green Branch	5 miles 0 furlongs 0 chains
Deanery Branch	3 miles 4 furlongs 6 chains
Stockton Branch	2 miles 3 furlongs 2 chains

The Construction of Norton Junction

Norton Junction was constructed in 1832 about 5 miles west of Port Clarence near Norton Toll Gate. The Toll Gate was situated on the corner of Junction Road and Blakeston Lane. The area was referred to as "Russell's Cut", perhaps named after Hamilton Russell, owner of a large amount of land in the area.. 400,000 cubic yards of ground were turned over in its creation. The engineer was Edward Steel (a protegé and early assistant of the Stephensons of Newcastle) under Christopher Tennant's guidance. In 1829 some of the other landowners involved had been distinctly unhappy, notably Messrs John and Jefferson Hogg of Norton House,overlooking Norton Green. They received only £2,100 for the 10½ acres requisitioned, against their initial expectations of £3,605.

The main line to Port Clarence ran over the valley between Norton and Billingham Bottoms. George Coates, the owner of Norton Mill, insisted on (and got) a 12ft wide bridge over his mill race at Billingham Beck rather than the intended 8ft bridge. The embankment at The Bottoms was 50ft, one of the highest built on the line, and still an impressive sight today. [George Coates was a Director in 1837 of the Bishop Auckland and Weardale Railway Company. His son, George Coates Jnr., was a Director in 1851 of the Wear Valley Railway Company.]

The first coals came down the Clarence line through Norton Junction to the staithes at Stockton in August 1833. The Clarence's own staithes at Stockton were ready in October 1833.

The Ticket Office and Waiting Room with Engine No.65817

THE END OF THE CLARENCE RAILWAY COMPANY

Unfortunately the restrictions by the S&DR Company at its junction at Sim Pasture, and the keen competition at Hartlepool Docks, meant that profits never reached expectations, and financial difficulties forced the leasing of the Clarence Railway Company. The Stockton and Hartlepool Railway Company (which had commenced its line in 1840 by a junction with the Clarence branch line near Billingham, running for about 8 miles to Hartlepool) leased the Clarence Railway Company in August 1844, for a period of 21 years. In January 1851 the line was leased in perpetuity to pay off other debts, and in June 1852 a Bill was passed to amalgamate under the Hartlepool Railway banner as the West Hartlepool Harbour and Railway Company. For most of its life the Clarence rail system was used mainly for goods and mineral traffic, passenger traffic being operated by the company for only about six months, before a private contractor took over the work. Only 20 years after its first horse-drawn wagons had trundled down the line the Clarence Railway Company no longer existed. However part of that line still exists at Norton Junction.

A locomotive steam engine stands at Norton Station

Ralph Ward Jackson of Hartlepool

Seal of The West Hartlepool Harbour and Railway Company

Christopher Tennant had been the instigator of plans for a Tees and Weardale Railway back in 1824 which were rejected, but his plans for the Clarence Railway Company were successful. He became involved with a great many projected railways (including the Great Northern) as well as ambitious plans to link the Clarence Railway with the expansion of Hartlepool Docks. His close friendship with Ralph Ward Jackson of Hartlepool (who became the founder of West Hartlepool, and after whom the prestigious Jacksons Landing and marina at Hartlepool are named) helped towards the accomplishment of some of Christopher Tennant's plans before his sudden demise in Leeds on 12th September 1839. (He is buried in the graveyard at Hartlepool's St Hilda's Church.) Mr Tennant had moved to Hartlepool in 1831 and, seeing the potential of Hartlepool's situation, proposed a link with his railway company. The new company was called the Stockton and Hartlepool Railway Company (S&HRC), although it was not incorporated until 1842. In May 1844 the S&HRC formed the Hartlepool West Harbour and Railway Company and in August 1844 the Clarence Railway Company was leased for 21 years to the S&HRC. By 1851 Ralph Ward Jackson controlled the Clarence Railway as well as the Stockton and Hartlepool Railway and the Hartlepool West Harbour and Dock Company. All of these companies amalgamated in June1852 and became known as the West Hartlepool Harbour and Railway Company. Christopher Tennant's ambitions were, posthumously, realised through his great friend.

Engine No.61220 arriving from Hartlepool

MESSRS FOSSICK AND HACKWORTH

The most significant development as far as Norton and its railway was concerned occurred around 1839/40. A small foundry, flour and saw mill on Norton Road was purchased by Mr George Fossick of Clapham and Mr Thomas Hackworth of Shildon with the intention of locomotive engine manufacture.

Mr George Fossick became an influential man locally. In the 1851 Census, Steam Engine Builder and Iron Founder George Fossick (a 41 year old bachelor) employed 231 men and boys, a fair sized establishment indeed. A large majority of those employed would of course come from both Norton and Stockton, so from the point of view of employment Fossick was an important man. It is interesting to note that on the day of the Census his two visitors were a Colliery Manager and a Railway Secretary.

Mr John Hackworth had been in charge of the engine building at Wylam (in County Durham) in the late 1700s, and when he died in 1810 his eldest son, Timothy (1786–July 1850) succeeded him. He left Wylam in 1815 and subsequently became the first Locomotive Superintendent of the S&DR at George Stephenson's request, establishing the Hackworth Soho Engine Works in Shildon (in which enterprise his brother Thomas ably assisted). Thomas Hackworth left the Shildon Works in 1839 to join with George Fossick at Stockton and took with him no small reputation for workmanship. No doubt the high respect with which Thomas Hackworth's family were regarded helped in the initial development, the high standard of workmanship being handed down from father to son.

Fossick and Hackworth's reputation ensured rapid expansion of their premises and workforce. Their engine and wagon building works secured contracts for passenger and mineral traffic haulage, as well as supplying locomotive engines and wagons to (among others) the S&DR Company, the Clarence Railway Company and the West Hartlepool Railway Company (until the merger in 1852).

Fossick and Hackworth's Steam Engine Building Manufactory

The company turned out around 100 locomotive and stationary engines, 72 of them prior to 1848 (4 of them for the Manchester, Sheffield and Lincoln line). The earliest engine delivered to the S&DR Company, on 9th June 1841, was called the *"Stockton"*. Locomotive engines and wagons were manufactured at the Norton Road Works until 1853, when a changeover to the new field of marine engines took place, under the management of Mr Robert Thorman. Two years later in 1855 Mr George Young Blair, a Scotsman, had taken over as Manager, and it was his unstinting exertions that enabled the firm to expand in this market.

In 1864 the Fossick and Hackworth partnership broke up, and on Thomas Hackworth's retirement the following year, the name was changed to Fossick and Blair. George Fossick's death in 1866 removed the last member of the original firm, and George Blair took over the 4½ acre site with a work force of over 700 under the name of Blair and Company Limited.

By the end of World War I, 1600 men and women were in Blair's employ, but by 1932 the factory had closed for good. In August 1933 the premises were purchased by a firm of timber and manufacturing joiners – F Hills and Sons. Throughout the 2nd World War, F Hills made fuselages and wings for the famous de Havilland "Mosquito" aircraft, known colloquially as "The Wooden Wonder".

The original steam engine building works were demolished in 1992. Although the remainder of the original premises is owned today by someone else, the premises are still locally referred to as "Hills".

North Shore and SH&C Stations

Just to the south of Fossick and Hackworth's Steam Engine Building Manufactory stood the Norton Road (North Shore) Junction Station of the Clarence Railway Company. It was built around 1835 for the first passengers, although it was 3 years before the first waiting room was built. The early stations, being built for economy rather than convenience, often had no platforms at all and certainly no shelter for the passengers.

In 1842 another station was built adjoining this one, for the Stockton and Hartlepool Railway Company (who leased the Clarence Railway Company two years later). This was designated the Stockton, Hartlepool and Clarence (SH&C) Passenger and Goods Railway Station, on Tilery Bank.

A directory for 1851 states that the Secretary of the SH&C Railway Company was Mr William Bassnett, the North Shore Stationmaster was Mr W M George Robinson, and the agent for the Goods Depot was Mr R Robinson. However, by the 1870s the station no longer catered for passengers, being used (for the next century or so) essentially for goods traffic and as a Parcels Office. The passenger traffic transferred over to the new station in Bishopton Lane, Stockton.

The station, its offices and the bridge carrying what was once the Clarence Company's main line to Stockton, were all razed to the ground some time in the mid-1970s. The site is now occupied by a small industrial estate with hi-tech units.

Fussick Bridge

Engine No.43108 passes over "Fuzzy bridge" and the "Blue bridge"

George Fossick died in 1866 but his time in Norton is remembered even today, for a bridge named after him is still very much in use. Situated just to the south of Norton Avenue, east of the Glebe Estate, Fossick's ("Fussick" or "Fuzzy") bridge is one of two erected to carry the Clarence railway line across Darlington Lane on its approach to Norton Junction. One was a cattle bridge, demolished in 1967 to make way for the Ring Road over which stands the "Blue bridge". The remaining small screw arch pedestrian/road bridge is now used as an access route between Norton Avenue and Dumbarton Avenue.

Just below the top ledge, in the centre of the bridge there used to be a small plaque with the date (1833) on, but it is now covered over with rendering and has been painted over with the date 1835!

Laying the track over "Fuzzy bridge"

EARLY RAIL TRAVEL

Horse-drawn travel

The "Union" railway coach used on the S&DR in 1836

On 11th July 1835 the first passengers were carried on the S&DR lines in waggonette-type horse-drawn coaches from Stockton to Coxhoe and back twice daily. 1st class travel meant a seat inside at a cost of 3/6d, and 2nd class passengers had to brave the outside elements for 2/6d. Two years later the Clarence Railway passenger trains were locomotive driven and the trip then cost 2/-d for outside and 2/6d for inside. Fares were usually collected on the trip by the guard, or even the engine driver, until tickets were introduced. On some lines the trains did not stop at a station unless the Stationmaster had a specific signal of some sort to tell the engine driver that there were any passengers to pick up. Woe betide the weary travellers at the mercy of an awkward Stationmaster! Bye-laws expressly prohibited passengers to smoke a pipe or cigar on the journey.

Locomotive travel

Passengers did not travel in the luxury of today's coaches – far from it. At first they travelled in goods wagons with seats. Blankets were sometimes provided to help reduce the effects of the cold draughts coming into the wagons from the holes in the floor, and through which the rain trickled. Some 3rd class carriages were simply open boxes without seats, so passengers travelled most uncomfortably standing shoulder to shoulder. At one time stage coaches were fitted with special wheels and used on the tracks but they proved more ornamental than practical, although it did make use of some of the stage coaches which had been forced off the roads due to the popularity of rail travel. It was not until the early 1870s that any form of heating for the coaches became widely used. Luggage, incidentally, was carried on top of the carriages.

A sight considered usual on the Clarence Railway was that of a train made up of passenger carriages attached to mineral and goods wagons, or goods wagons and sheep trucks attached to passenger carriages.

A Commuter's Tale

An interesting piece of information detailing the trials and tribulations of 19th century commuting was passed on to me by a local historian and is well worth a mention here, as one of the stopping-off points was the North Shore Junction Station.

During the 1840's, anyone travelling from Newcastle to London must have arrived at their destination in a rather bemused condition and not a little the worse for wear. The marathon would begin with a stage coach trip from Newcastle, over the Tyne to Gateshead, then a train journey to Monkwearmouth. Another stagecoach journey to Sunderland Station, then a train ride, eventually ending up at North Shore Junction Station. A short coach trip from there took the traveller to the Bridge Road Station, and from there another train took him, via Normanton in the Midlands, to his destination of London. Necessity alone must have surely been the watchword to undertake a journey like that!!

Railway Workers

In the early 1840's all railway servants, regardless of class, worked long hours for comparatively small remuneration, moreover their duties were not clearly defined. Weekly wages would be similar to the following:

Engineman	24/-d to 30/-d
Fireman	15/-d to 18/-d
Guard	24/-d to 26/-d
Porter	17/-d to 22/-d
Policeman or Switchman	17/-d to 20/-d
Platelayer	18/-d to 19/-d
Carriage cleaner	15/-d to 16/-d
Coke Filler	15/-d to 18/-d

Engine drivers were paid 0.1875d per ton per mile for all coals carried. Although repairs to engines were the responsibility of the Company, the drivers provided their own firemen and had to find coals, fire bars, oil, lamps etc. One of the fireman's more hazardous duties was to brake the wagons on a downhill run, by putting the engine out of gear and letting down the wagon brakes, then returning to his post on the engine by hopping along the top of the coals from wagon to wagon.

There was no job demarcation as such – enginemen filled tenders, firemen acted as pointsmen, moving the switches (shift rails) manually, and booking clerks acted as guards.

An inspector or superintendent of police could earn up to £78 per annum, with a uniform provided and sometimes a lodging allowance.

Stationmasters had very little status and worked 14 hours a day, often 7 days a week. The master of a terminal station could earn up to £100 a year, the master of a small station £60 to £80. At first a Stationmaster's house was not provided. The Clarence rail system at Sedgefield in 1840 was run from a public house (the "Stag and Dragon") and mine host was the Stationmaster.

"Railway Mania"

From Norton Junction, passengers could travel west to Darlington and then on to Leeds, east to Hartlepool, or south to Stockton. The Junction came into its own as a place of note while "railway mania" swept the country during the 1840s. Fortunes were made by speculators and shareholders as the iron road spread over the whole country, not only proving financially viable to speculators of all classes, but also of great advantage to ordinary men and women who wanted to see more of the country in which they lived.

"Railway mania" had taken hold to such an extent that by 1852 more than 6,000 miles of railway track had been laid down and 73 million passengers had been conveyed by the various companies. This was no mean feat when the early railways had been condemned as dangerous because of the popular belief that it was physically impossible for a human body to travel faster than 20 mph!!

The Cheap Trains Act of 1846 stated that at least one train every day on every line must carry passengers at only 1d per mile. Queen Victoria encouraged their use by frequent rail travel from the 1840s, proving that the new form of travel was by no means only for the lower classes.

The Crystal Palace Exhibition in 1851

A great many people followed Queen Victoria's example, and in 1851 over 6 million people used the railways to go and see the Great Exhibition in The Crystal Palace in London's Hyde Park. This was a great fair set up in a huge exhibition hall to show exhibits from all over the world, an idea thought up by Prince Albert, Queen Victoria's husband. Joseph Paxton was the architect and he designed the building as a huge railway station, made of iron and glass, and $^{3}/_{4}$ of a mile in length. Railway navvies erected it and the rail companies ran cheap fare excursion trains from all over the country. The whole thing was a huge success, due primarily to the co-operation of the rail people in putting up the building and in bringing the country folk to see it.

Norton Junction played a minor part in this success, for many Nortonians would also have been spectators, bringing back a memento or two. One visitor to the Great Exhibition brought back a case of books (12 volumes in all) entitled "The History of Great Britain 1851". These volumes were found in one of the rooms during the restoration work of No. 32 High Street, Norton, still in their original case and in pristine condition. An inscription on the flyleaf of the first volume testified that they were indeed from the Great Exhibition in London.

NORTON JUNCTION

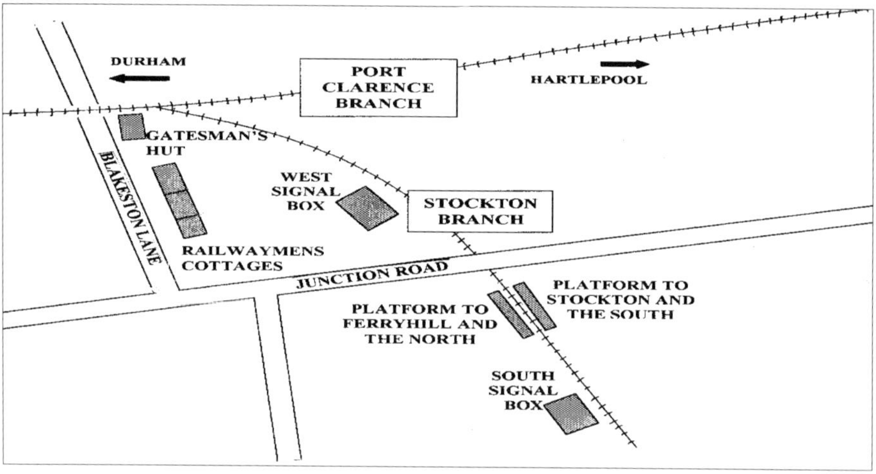

The map above gives an indication of how Norton Junction looked in the 1830s with the original platforms and west signal box.

The map below shows the development of Norton Junction 50 years later. The platforms and west signal box were re-positioned and the new east curve was added.

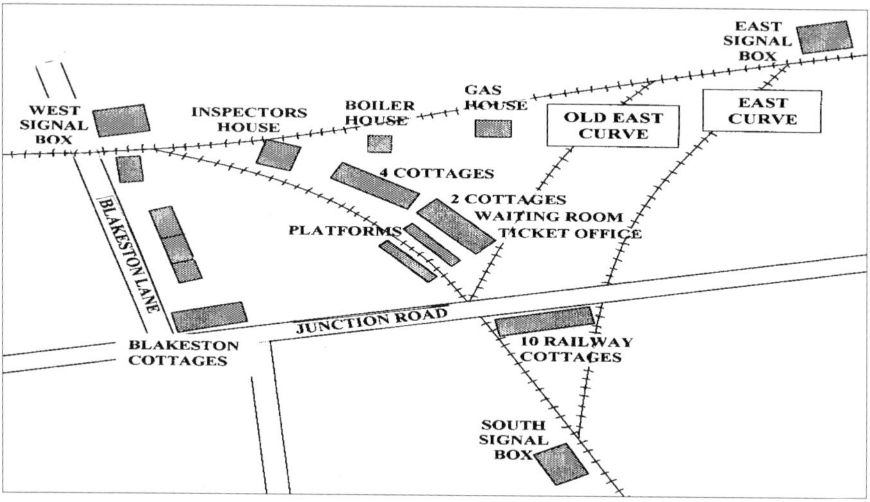

Norton Junction and its Early Buildings

In 1833 Norton Junction consisted of just 2 signal cabins, a gatesman's hut and a row of 3 small cottages on Blakeston Lane (no entry was available at that time from Junction Road). The 1841 Census Forms tell us that these 3 cottages were the homes of the Gatekeeper, Engineman Thomas Laing and his family, and Railway Inspector Thomas Bell and his family (wife Barbara and 7 children ranging in age from 2 days to 14 years). Imagine the overcrowding in that house!

Development of the junction "triangle" began to take place when the Stockton and Hartlepool Railway Company leased the line in 1842, and it was considered that a new curve to the east of that in use would facilitate more easily those trains travelling to and from the Hartlepool routes. This is shown on the map as the "old east curve".

New stone platforms were erected around 1837 to the north of the original ones, over Junction Road, and a "terrace" built to accommodate a Ticket Room and Waiting Room for passengers' comfort, plus a row of 6 workers' cottages. There was also a water tower, coal drops, signal and track maintenance sheds, a gas house and a boiler house.

There was a small shop selling the basics within the Junction "triangle". However, with the frequency of trains the residents found it easier to get to Stockton market than into Norton Village. This self-sufficiency made the "triangle" a community on its own.

Later on, to the south of Norton Junction a terrace of 10 workers' cottages were built by the NER for the men who worked for the railway. This way the workforce would be on hand when needed rather than be isolated outside the "triangle. These are known today as Nos. 2 to 11 Railway Cottages.

Residents at Norton Junction

The houses at Norton Junction changed tenants fairly rapidly, apart from the Bell family who were living there in 1841 until at least 1871. The Census Forms for 1851 show that there had indeed been some expansion at the junction, for 6 residences are listed (though one was uninhabited), occupied by men and their families from outside of Norton. Notable amongst these was 60 year old William Robson, a Journeyman Joiner from Shildon (possibly a "Hackworth employee"), and 34 year old Thomas Brown (also a Journeyman Joiner) from Yorkshire. 35 year old Robert Harrison (yet another Journeyman Joiner) and 57 year old railway labourer William Proud (classed as an agricultural labourer on the previous census) were both Norton-born men. By this time, 49 year old Yorkshireman Thomas Bell was a railway Inspector, and he and wife Barbara and their large family of 9 children would probably have been living in the Inspector's House. (The Census Forms for 1841 tell us there were 7 children to Mr and Mrs Bell.)

The first Stationmaster mentioned as living at the junction (1861) was George Arundale, a 47 year old bachelor living with his 82 year old widowed mother. Certainly there are no other references to a master living at Norton Junction, perhaps they had lived in the village. By the late 1870s Henry Burcombe of Page Terrace was Stationmaster at the "halt" down Calf Fallow Lane, succeeded in 1895 by Henry Parkin, also of Page Terrace.

"Woodbine Cottages" on Blakeston Lane, were possibly built as an 'overflow' from the Junction Cottages. The two tiny houses were the homes of a Foreman at the Blast Furnace, and an engine driver and his family.

"Blakeston Cottages" had been built by 1881 (on the corner of Blakeston Lane and Junction Road). For a time one of these houses was used as a Toll Cottage, for Blakeston Lane marked the end of the parish of Norton and this road led up to Sedgefield. People coming into and out of the parish had to pay a toll as a form of tax, which helped to pay some of the people who repaired or laid roads. While the junction cottages have now been demolished, the terrace of 10 cottages to the south of Junction Road, and Blakeston cottages still stand today.

The former Waiting Room/Ticket Office (shown in the two sketches below) was converted into a Methodist Chapel around 1877, with a nominal rent of 1s 0d per year, to seat 30 to 40. The congregation consisted mainly of railway and furnace workers, plus farmers and their labourers from the farms outside the village. The pulpit and the piano stood on a raised platform and the building was heated by an open fire on the east wall of the room. Many people still fondly remember the Christmas Carol concerts and Harvest Festivals, the Easter services and the prize givings. The Sunday School made many trips from the junction to Seaton Carew. The chapel was closed in 1948 when a new one was built at Ragworth - the congregation had dwindled to 6 people and did not warrant keeping the Junction Chapel open any longer. The last preacher was Rev. Norman Teklaw and the steward/churchwarden was Mr Thomas Towl.

In 1841 an inn had been listed at Norton Junction, run by Thomas Hardy and his wife, with a female servant. This suggested that a public house existed on the site, but in all probability this was simply a case of using the "front room" of one of the cottages, rather than a purpose-built inn (as has been the case with some of the alehouses in the village). Certainly there was a lot of pressure brought to bear on the railway companies by Revivalist Campaigners to ban the sale of alcoholic drinks to both passengers and labourers, due to a number of accidents on the railways having occurred as a result of the "demon drink". Perhaps this was the case here, for the Clarence Railway Company would have been subject to pressure too.

The Inspector's House

The Inspector's house shown below was built at a later date, a short distance from the "service" area. Gas supply lines were laid and a Gas House and Boiler House built. 57 year old John Wright was the Inspector by 1881 and he was the last railway employee to live in the Inspector's House. After Norton Station down Cross-Dike Lane had been built in the 1870s, the Junction gradually declined, the buildings were sold off or rented out and the area took on a different role.

A number of the original buildings at Norton Junction were demolished in October 1981. At this time, the Inspector's House was occupied by Don Wardale and his family. The remains of a couple of buildings, one of which was formerly used as the Boiler House, still serve as a reminder of the Junction's past. Gas lamps were still in use in the house right up until 1992, when electricity was introduced.

The Inspector's House and the building shown to the left of the photograph, previously used as the Boiler House, are now listed buildings. The house now belongs to Don Wardale's daughter and her husband, who are undertaking extensive restoration.

The Inspector's House in the early 1990s taken from near the west signal box

Excursions and Holidays from Norton Junction

A locomotive arriving at the Ticket Office at Norton Junction.
The Inspector's House is to the left of the picture

Towards the end of the 19th Century such was the impact of the wider distribution of food and fresh produce to all areas and all classes through rail transport, that an improvement was noted in health and attitudes. The frequent trains enabled many people to live away from their place of work, and to take frequent holidays away. The working classes who could not afford a holiday away took day excursions to the local seaside resorts and into the country, special trains often being laid on to cope with demand.

The long hot summers (it always seemed to be sunny in days gone by!) and the new-found accessibility of "the seaside" enabled trainloads of famili es to escape for the day from the rigours of town living and the smog of encroaching industrialisation. Excited youngsters waving buckets and spades, mums and dads laden with food hampers and rugs and all sorts of paraphernalia all crowded noisily and happily into the carriages to be taken to Seaton Carew (the nearest seaside resort) or into the country, and the junction swarmed like a beehive. The railway companies advertised the virtues of rail travel and when the actual outing day came, excitement was at fever pitch.

Sunday School trips to Seaton Carew were also a regular occurrence, for there were several Sunday Schools in the area and the resort was only a short journey away. Harassed teachers and helpers must have been worn out at the end of the day trying to keep their herd of bucket-and-spade-waving youngsters together, for they would inevitably all want to do something different. Some would want to go and get an ice cream, some to look around the shops, some to the amusement booths, some to go swimming in the cool sea and some to build sandcastles. The young ladies would be made to keep on their wide-brimmed bonnets because it was considered unwise to allow the complexion to be spoiled by direct contact with the sun (freckles were considered unsightly), while "boys would be boys" and were allowed a bit more freedom. The train journey home must have been a nightmare, though I am sure everyone had enjoyed themselves immensely. Sadly, the last Sunday School trip to leave Norton Junction took place in 1913.

Special trains were laid on during the Durham Miners Gala Day (a strictly men-only affair, with colliery brass bands and marching parades). The women and children were taken out somewhere for the day, for this day was classed as a statutory holiday, and everyone made the most of it.

Specials were also laid on to Stockton, operating on Saturdays from 9 a.m. to 3 p.m. and many women made a day of it, taking dinner along for themselves and their children. These were nicknamed the "Housewives' Specials".

Royalty At Norton Junction

Royalty, however, always aroused interest and Norton's Junction was no exception. Here the 'excitement quota' reached its zenith between the 1880s and the early 1900s when it was patronised by His Royal Highness The Prince of Wales, "Bertie" as he was popularly known (Queen Victoria's eldest son and heir, later King Edward VII). The close proximity of Norton Junction to Lord Londonderry's estate at Wynyard was the prime reason for his visits through Norton Junction. Although a station had been built at Wynyard, it never proved popular with either the visiting VIPs or the railway companies. Because it was a 'blank end' station, much shunting, stopping and re-routing of trains was required to divert trains through Thorpe Thewles, Carlton, etc. during special visits. As royal trains had priority, this meant a break in the heavy traffic (especially coal) using the routes, much to the disturbance of the ship owners and officers who were keen on catching the earliest possible tides. Norton Junction was on a direct line from London to Newcastle at this time, and any royal or special VIP coach could be slotted in between regular rail traffic – so everyone was happy.

Some of the visiting guests to Wynyard to pass through Norton Junction included ambassadors of varying degrees. The Imperial Emperor of China (with pigtails and jewels and gorgeous silk robes), ambassadors from the court of the Csar of Russia (with fur caps and voluminous greatcoats), Russian Cossack officers (with fur mittens and soft leather knee boots), and other ministers and statesmen of a multitude of countries, on missions of business and pleasure.

One of the duties of the Inspector was to ensure that additional staff was available during VIP travel from the junction, but one particular train caused more than the usual chaos and disorder.

It was in 1884 when a telegram arrived at Wynyard to inform Lord Londonderry that HRH the Prince of Wales would be arriving "after Ebor" (York), signed by the Prince's A.D.C. Ponsonby. Lord Londonderry did not panic, for the imminent arrival of his friend and future king was no longer a disturbance, his visits were actually rather frequent. In 30 years

Edward, as Prince and as King visited Wynyard 28 times, usually on what is termed as "very private visits indeed".

All was the usual hustle and bustle as coaches and carriages were made ready to receive the VIP guests, and a couple of carts were cleaned and polished for the servants and the luggage. At approximately 6.30 p.m. the special train arrived at Norton Junction and the Marquis stepped forward to greet his royal friend, to be greeted by the sight of not 2 carriages discharging visitors but 5! for the Prince had brought "a few friends" to share his lordship's hospitality. Panic must have set in now for how were they all to be conveyed to Wynyard with so little transport available? When the Prince and some of his entourage clattered out of Norton Junction a distraught Stationmaster and Inspector sent young lads down to Norton Station and to the big houses in the village to beg the use of any available transport, for no fewer than 90 had arrived in the distinguished party – and that was without their servants! What the young bloods of St. James must have thought on being taken to Wynyard in the cabs and carts hurriedly assembled for their use (some bearing the name of the tradesmen who loaned them), with their luggage following in farm and fruit wagons, can only be imagined. Certainly it was different!

On this occasion, as on most occasions when guests arrived at Wynyard, several servants were 'pressed' into service from Norton's big houses to help in the kitchens or dining rooms, and sometimes to act as ladies' maids, although many guests brought their own gentleman or lady dresser.

Apparently 'Bertie' treated the workers at Norton and Wynyard Stations on a par with grooms or the lowest order of servants. An unpolished boot remarked upon brought down the wrath of everyone from the railway directors downward, sometimes with disastrous results. Many of the gentry were poor tippers and followed the example set by their Prince, so that VIP visits sometimes resulted in rather reluctant service.

King Edward VII was not the only royal personage to use Norton Junction though. In 1953, the new Queen Elizabeth II and her husband the Duke of Edinburgh passed through the junction during their coronation tour. The Royal Train stood in the cutting against Summerville Farm (near Sainsbury's) overnight before continuing the journey to Newcastle.

NORTON STATION

The station at Norton-on-Tees should not be confused with Norton Junction, which is actually $^{1}/_{2}$ mile to its west.

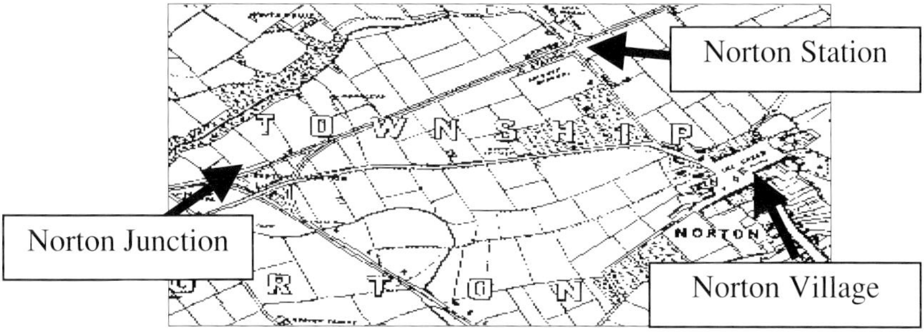

Norton Station ("The Halt")

The "halt" was originally built $^{1}/_{2}$ mile to the east of Norton Junction to cater for the traffic to Warner, Lucas and Barrett's Iron Works, down Cross-Dike Lane. (The Iron Works famously produced Big Ben's bell in August 1856). By the late 1870s this had been developed to encompass a station, with extra sidings and platforms to take the vast amounts of coal, coke and iron ore being delivered to and from the works. By 1881 this station had superseded the original station and the decline of Norton Junction had begun.

Train arriving at Norton-on-Tees Station

The Station Inn

In 1851 Norton Station Inn is listed at the "halt" down Calfallow Lane, down Cross-Dike Lane (now Station Road). This was run by John Hardy, farmer and innkeeper. He previously lived at Hornletts Farm (off Junction Road), and he appears to have taken over a sizeable property. Here lived his wife and 3 of his 6 children as well as his son-in-law John Hall (a locomotive engine driver from Sunderland who formerly lodged with William Proud of Norton Junction). There were 2 lodgers, one an engine driver and one a stoker. John Hardy was 70 in 1871. In 1881, 40 year old John Galilee had succeeded John Hardy as publican and farmer.

The Station Inn (later Hotel), not surprisingly, became popular with the passengers who used the 'halt', which was really just a platform used as a dropping off point. It was also frequented by the many workers from the nearby farms and the Iron Works. Many a parched throat had been given the 'kiss of life' after a hard day working near the furnaces. The inn has survived despite the several recessions in its lifetime and is now called The Norton Tavern.

Steam Engine passing Norton Station on the right. The Stationmaster's House can be seen in the centre of the picture

FROM STEAM TO DIESEL

Norton Junction (Development of Railway Operations)

To fully understand the operation of the Junction, it is necessary to take an overall look at the north-east railway system.

In the early days the most important route was the Norton West–Norton East line (the "back line") but as will clearly be seen this is no longer the case. This stretch of the line is now by far the least used of the three routes which make up Norton Junction. From its origins as part of the Clarence Railway Company's (alternative) link between the Durham coalfields and the mouth of the River Tees, the Junction rapidly became swallowed up in the northward advance of the Leeds Northern Railway (formerly the Thirsk and Leeds Railway).

The Leeds Northern Railway reached Stockton from the south via Northallerton and Sedgefield, having officially opened on 15th May 1852. The company's new station in Bishopton Road, Stockton, opened on 2nd June of that year, joining the Clarence Railway at what became known as the North Shore Junction on Norton Road. This opened the junction for use as a through route, enabling the Leeds Northern trains to use the west curve to gain the Clarence route as far as Stillington, and then on to Ferryhill where the main route to the north could be joined.

A further development of Norton Junction came about on 1st March 1880 when the North Eastern Railway Company (NER) opened a line from Bowesfield Junction (Stockton) northwards through Thorpe Thewles to join the existing Hartlepool-Haswell-Sunderland line. A link curve installed at Carlton East Junction allowed trains on this new route to join the Clarence line to Norton Junction, and so gain access via the Leeds Northern Station at Stockton. This route was used by Newcastle-Liverpool expresses until the opening of the coast route via Hartlepool.

The completion of this coast route between Hartlepool and Sunderland in 1905 enabled through running of Newcastle-Liverpool express trains via

Hartlepool and Stockton, so avoiding the notorious bank at Seaton on the Wellfield-Ryhope line, although for a number of years at least one daytime express continued on this route. Thus, for a while, Norton Junction saw Newcastle-Liverpool expresses using both the east and west curves on regular timings!

Local services through Norton Junction were provided by Stockton-Coxhoe and Stockton-Port Clarence trains in the early days, but as the network of lines in the area increased, services such as Newcastle-Middlesbrough/Saltburn/Whitby were added to passenger workings.

One point of interest to note is the siting of the platforms at this junction. Only the original platforms of 1835 were capable of serving trains on both east and west curves. Once the platforms were re-sited to the north of the road bridge and the new east curve installed, Norton Junction Station was unable to serve the increasingly busy east curve coast route. Was this the reason for the development of Station Road, and thus the eventual demise of Norton Junction Station?

Freight traffic developed rapidly with the advancement of the railway network in the north-east so that, following on from the original coal traffic between Shildon and Haverton Hill/Port Clarence, the junction soon found itself catering for coal traffic between Shildon and the growing iron industry at Middlesbrough on the south bank of the River Tees.

The opening by the NER in 1877 of the first stretch of the Bowesfield-Wellfield line between Bowesfield (Stockton) and Carlton West Junction provided the Shildon area with this more direct outlet for its coal to the Middlesbrough area without having to use either Norton Junction or the busy stretch of line to Stockton.

However by this time the junction was becoming host to another source of coal traffic. The mining of coal was gradually moving away from inland pits to coastal and as a result traffic was being generated from new directions to pass through Norton on its way to the heart of the iron works on the south bank of the Tees. On opening a final link between Hartlepool and Sunderland in 1905, the coastal collieries had a direct link to the industrial Tees as well as outlets for the finished products from these industries.

Directly related to the coal traffic was the iron ore/iron product traffic which used all routes through the junction. The east curve was used by trains conveying ore from (originally) the mines of North Yorkshire and (later) the Middlesbrough docks to the Hartlepool iron works. The west curve and the "back line" handled trains carrying finished products from both the Hartlepool and Middlesbrough works to customers in the Northern Regions.

Engine No. 63432 at Norton Station

Railway Operations from 1960

The 1960s began a period of great change for the British Railway network. The Beeching "axe" was about to fall on many rural lines, and the change in motive power from steam to diesel was well under way. Norton Junction remained relatively unchanged throughout the decade although evidence of change was discernible on examination of the various routes passing through it.

The first major change to be seen here came in the form of diesel railcars which were introduced in increasing numbers throughout the country during the late 1950s. These railcars replaced the tank engine and two/three carriage combinations which were once a familiar sight trundling through Norton Junction, taking over the local services along the coast route between Newcastle, Hartlepool, Middlesbrough and Stockton, and were also to be seen on the Newcastle-Leeds services which used the coastal route.

Diesel locomotives started to appear around the Junction from 1959. At first the larger main line locos appeared but as production increased the smaller locos intended for local passenger/freight working were allocated to the various loco depots around the area. It was quite common during the early 1960s to see a brand-new diesel locomotive on a test run from the railway workshops at Darlington North Road passing through Norton Junction.

Steam locos maintained a strong foothold in the north-east until 1967 when the last few loco depots lost their allocation of steam engines to the scrap merchants. This transition period from steam to diesel power made Norton Junction a very interesting place to be during the 1960s for the keen loco spotter, certainly from the point of view of railway traffic variety

Train pulling through the road bridge over Norton Junction's East Curve

EAST CURVE
(Norton South–Norton East)

This curve carried the heaviest flow of traffic, indeed a seemingly endless flow in both directions of freight trains carrying coal/iron ore/finished products, interspersed with local and express passenger trains.

Passenger trains on this curve consisted of local workings such as Newcastle-Middlesbrough and Hartlepool-Darlington services, all of which were in the charge of diesel railcars or the express trains using the coast route between Newcastle and Stockton.

Up until 1963 most of the London expresses on a secondary route such as this would be powered by Gresley passenger locos from classes A4, A3, A2 and A1 until they were gradually replaced by diesel locos. The cross-country and holiday trains used a mixed bag of locos but mainly those from passenger/goods classes such as V2, B1 engines, with diesels taking over at a date later than on the London expresses.

Goods trains on the east curve continued using steam locos up until 1964/65 when diesel classes became more used, but even so some steam engines could still be seen working through Norton Junction up until September 1967, when the Hartlepool depot finally closed to steam, making diesel engines the only power available.

Engine No.90067 passing Norton East signal box

WEST CURVE
(Norton South–Norton West)

This curve went through a period of mixed fortunes during the 1960s. Through the week it was used very little except for a few local freight trains and some transfer freight between the industrial areas of Teesside and Tyneside.

Where it really came into its own was on a weekend when maintenance work on the East Coast main line between Northallerton and Darlington resulted in all the main line traffic being diverted through Stockton and Stillington. From midnight on a Saturday until midnight on a Sunday the west curve was used by express trains for destinations literally all round the country.

A look at a railway timetable for the summer of 1963 shows traffic on the west curve, for example, as 40 main line expresses within 24 hours, not including parcel and freight trains! The signalman at Norton South Junction must have been very busy indeed, especially as he also had to contend with the workings using the east curve!

Motive power on these express trains brought some very famous engines to Norton Junction; the Gresley A4s and A3s (such as *"Mallard"*, A4; *"Sir Nigel Gresley"*, A4; and *""The Flying Scotsman"*, A3) as well as the 'Deltic' diesel engines. All of these engines have now disappeared from the railways of Britain.

Engine No.90588 passing Norton west signal box

"THE BACK LINE"
(Norton West–Norton East)

This link line did not see any regular passenger service for decades, if at all during the latter part of the 20th Century, as traffic was restricted entirely to freight. It was quite common, however, to see a train waiting at Norton East Junction unable to get a "path" on the coast line between Stockton and Billingham because of the heavy traffic on that route.

The "back line" has never actually fallen into complete disuse, although the track is overgrown with weeds and gives the impression of being abandoned, all the more saddening to recall its one-time importance.

An interesting feature of this "back line" is the number of sidings which were lifted in the late 1960s. They were used in the early part of that decade to store condemned rolling stock, the lines behind the Inspector's House storing old carriages, whilst the sidings nearer the east junction once hosted a group of redundant steam engines awaiting the breaker's torch.

Engine No. 60876 on the "back line" passing Norton-on-Tees signal box

DECLINE OF THE JUNCTION

The introduction of diesel power onto the national rail network was only part of an overall modernisation plan, which as well as updating the railway equipment in general also affected freight and passenger operations.

Apart from the new motive power that could be seen working through Norton Junction, however, little change was evident during the late 1960s. Some redundant equipment was removed, such as the sidings that lay to the north of the "back line" (east to west link) and the siding, which branched from the west curve and served the original Junction Station. Also, the reversal cross-over lines which were situated at each signal box were removed as surplus to requirements.

A new bridge was installed to the north of the original Fussick bridge (an operation which took a full weekend to accomplish and which was witnessed by a very large crowd of onlookers). Also, the bridge over the west curve was strengthened, the original metal side plates being replaced by brick walls.

Most of the railway equipment to be seen today at Norton Junction has been in use for nearly 70 years, and all the signalling is carried out by manual semaphore signals operated from the three signal boxes around the junction. Some of the equipment still carries the LNER (London North Eastern Railway) symbol, and one signal (situated 20 yards west of the Inspector's House) is still mounted on a wooden post – definitely a relic from much earlier than the time of railway nationalisation in 1948. One piece of modern equipment which seems out of place is the continental-style crossing gates spanning Blakeston Lane at the Norton West signal box. These replaced earlier manually-operated wooden gates which were demolished by a diesel hauled freight train on 9th September 1969 when the gates failed to open fully to allow the passage of the train!

Two housing estates have been built adjacent to the junction, one at each side of the Junction triangle. The first was built in a field to the south of the east junction, covering a cart track which provided access to the wood at the north of the junction (known locally as Ozzy, or Fozzy Wood). The track crossed the railway by means of a gated crossing which, although still in situ, has fallen out of use through its inaccessibility. The second, newer, estate (Blakeston Court) was built in the field behind the cottages at the entrance to Blakeston Lane. This estate partly removed traces of a cart track which ran off the present Junction Road and led to a railway crossing just to the north of the present road bridge. Traces of the crossing can still be seen, as well as remains of the cart track which runs parallel to the road, following the hedge, all overgrown of course. This could possibly have been the original road prior to the building of the present road bridge over the west curve.

Passenger traffic through the junction went into decline during the late 1960s, and was first evident with the withdrawal of some express trains which for years had used the Leeds Northern route through Norton in preference to the main East Coast line between Newcastle, Darlington and Northallerton. By the mid-1970s all but two of these trains had been withdrawn or transferred to the Darlington route, leaving Norton Junction served by local feeder services between Hartlepool and Darlington. The two express trains that remained were the Newcastle-London sleeper service, and the return working, both trains of only two or three coaches which were attached or detached from the main train (which used the Darlington line) at Darlington, and worked through Stockton to serve those stations along the coast route.

Freight services too were reduced dramatically, due primarily to the recession and rundown of British industry. Both coal and iron ore (traditionally regarded as the mainstay of the north east freight services) suffered badly because of the recession, and this reflected on Norton Junction. The west curve was severely affected by the shutdown of the Consett Steelworks, as this line formed part of a link between the steel complexes of Middlesbrough and Redcar and the Consett works.

However, the oil industry brought some welcome revenue to the railways of Teesside. The original Clarence Railway branch to Haverton Hill and Port Clarence provided an outlet for the products from the refineries at Seal Sands, so that regular train loads of oil and associated products could be seen using the lines once predominantly coal-oriented.

After the Decline

During 1914 the 5th Battalion of the Territorial Corps (the C.R.E.) ran Norton Junction for intense training of personnel for a period of 3 months during mobilisation prior to operations in France.

In the 1930s Sentinel Steam Coaches ran on this line for a number of years from Newcastle to Middlesbrough, but their lack of coal-carrying capacity for fuel meant they were taken out of service after a few embarrassing unscheduled stops.

Also in the 1930s, new locomotives for the LNER ran from Stockton to Norton Junction on a 'test run' to see how they operated on curves. The LNER Engineer at this time was Sir Nigel Gresley, designer of the famous ***"Flying Scotsman"***.

Between 1939 and 1945 (The Second World War) the Royal Army Ordnance Corps (R.A.O.C.) built a spur line, operating to the nearby Ammunition Store and Dump (formerly timber and builders merchants Crossleys, now Jewson). One of the underground Ferro-concrete bunkers and part of the line still exist today.

Local passenger services using the east curve were under the threat of heavy, crippling cutbacks or even total withdrawal, while freight traffic (on the decrease and with the threat to the area's steel industries looking grim) also seemed doomed.

Rumours circulated for some time of plans to modernise Norton Junction's layout and install colour light signalling controlled from the Norton West cabin (although this would mean the closure of both the South and East boxes).

During the mid-1970s there was a proposal to create a station at Roseworth to encourage people to use the rail network as a means of commuting to Stockton and Middlesbrough. If Norton Junction had been kept open, people would have been doing that anyway, since the housing estates spread out from the centre of Stockton in the early 1950s.

The west curve is used mainly these days when the main line is closed for repair or maintenance work, so that traffic is infrequent. When the 125s and modern fast trains do use this route, they are obliged to slow down considerably to avoid damaging the old tracks, for they were never designed or built for the high speeds at which today's trains flash past.

It is a certainty, however, that few of the passengers on these trains, or the visitors to Harper's Garden Centre nearby, are aware that this is in fact one of the oldest railway junctions - not only in Britain but in the world.

****

Norton Junction's history is well worth recording. It may have lost its importance, and most of its buildings may have been demolished, but let us not allow it to be forgotten completely.

****

We reproduce on the next page a Norton farmer's poem expressing regret at the take-over of his farm to make way for a railway development.

Blackroods Farm by Gretta Percy

A FARMER'S LAMENT

I've lost my farm, I do declare!
A Railway Yard is "in the air",
"Compulsory Purchase", Government say
"But compensation we will pay".

Landmark for years on all the maps
"Blackroods" not much to average chaps
"Time it was down" the critics say
And all at once I feel at bay.

The whispering corn half ripened there
The bobbing tail of a hard pressed hare,
The startled partridge taking wing,
Hurray! a shotgun missing the thing.

Peewit and redshank too are there
Such pleading cry, just like a prayer.
Sweet throated thrush in yonder tree
"Tough cheese", "tough cheese",
he sings to me.

As men moved in with charges fused,
My mind ran back – let's see, I mused.
A drain is blocked, get a spade and spit,
Go and clean it out a bit.

Lambing time, all baa baa baa,
In and out of bed we are.
Soon lambs frisking in the lea
Delightful sight indeed to see.

It's drying up, get harrows bright,
Time to sow, the land is white.
Tatties in, its March you know,
Time to start to make 'em grow.

Turnips next, and then the seeds,
Don't forget to spray the weeds.
Hoeing done, then time to rest,
July weather at its best.

Haytime comes with breakneck speed
Cut it down when it's in seed.
Turn it, thump it into bale,
Get it sold – if it's for sale.

Harvest here with golden grain,
Hope it doesn't start to rain.
Combine going, corn into bin,
Soon all safely gathered in.

October here I dread to say,
Tattie time is on the way.
Must be done like all the rest,
Get 'em up! As you know best.

By xmas ploughing done with zeal,
Wet as mush or dry as meal.
Get it up to get the frost,
That's the rule at any cost.

Awakened from this daylight dream,
Attention drawn to present scheme!
I stood and watched the stackyard go,
Bulldozeer laid the stable low.

Tear in eye, down went the lot,
Including yellow chimney pot.
Big cloud of dust waved up on high
As if to bid me last goodbye.

Too late I fear for pastures new,
I'm t'other side of sixty-two.
Must be content with hard earned
gains,
Sit and watch the Liner trains.

Mr Charles Harland Thompson of Blackroods Farm, which was demolished in 1971

THE CLARENCE AND ASSOCIATED RAILWAYS - A CHRONOLOGY

The Clarence Railway (Port Clarence Branch). This line was built primarily for the transportation of coal from the newly-opened south-west Durham collieries, for shipment from both Stockton and Hartlepool. The line later attracted traffic connected with shipbuilding and iron-based trades. The Company was incorporated in 1828 (founder Christopher Tennant of Yarm) and absorbed into the West Hartlepool Harbour and Railway Company in 1852, then merged with the North Eastern Railway Company in 1865.

1768 - Robert Whitworth's survey into a canal from Winston to Stockton proved too expensive to implement.

1810 - **10th September** – Opening of the Mandale Cut of the River Tees at Stockton. At this meeting Leonard Raisbeck advocated the need for a canal or railway to link up with the south west Durham collieries, a far-reaching proposal which did not come to fruition until 1825 with the creation of the Stockton and Darlington Railway Company.

1812 - James Rennie's canal survey using Robert Whitworth's route also proved financially unacceptable.

1818 - George Overton carried out a survey regarding the feasibility of a railway connecting to the Durham coalfields.
July - Report published by Christopher Tennant on the proposed canal from the river Tees to the coal district of West Auckland, taking in the beck along Billingham/Norton Bottoms. Rejected in **October 1818**.
13th November – George Overton's finding in favour of a railway was accepted. A prospectus was issued to form the S&DR.
George Stephenson undertook a new survey regarding a railway to the collieries.

1819 - The Bill to build a railway was defeated.

1820 - **12th February** – A meeting was held in The George & Dragon Hotel in Yarm High Street, presided over by Thomas Meynell of Yarm to promote the Stockton & Darlington Railway, the first public railway in the world.

1821 - **19th April** – The Bill finally gained Royal Assent allowing a line for the S&DR from Witton Park in County Durham to Stockton in County Durham, with 5 branches. At this time the railway was primarily expected to transport raw materials. Passengers had not been thought of yet. At this time Edward Pease of Darlington was the most important businessman involved financially with the S&DR.
May – Thomas Meynell of Yarm was elected Chairman of the S&DR.

1822 – **22nd January** – George Stephenson appointed Engineer to the Stockton & Darlington Railway Company.
23rd May – The first rail of the Stockton & Darlington Railway was laid at St John's Well, Bridge Road, Stockton, by Thomas Meynell.

1823 - **23rd May** – An Act was given Royal Assent to transport passengers on the S&DR.

1824 - **September** – 2 locomotives ordered by the Stockton & Darlington Railway Company – *"Locomotion"* and *"Hope"*.

1825 - **27th September** – George Stephenson's *"Locomotion"* pulled the leading train on the opening day of The Stockton & Darlington Railway Company, from Shildon in County Durham to Darlington. The journey was 9 miles long and took 2 hours to complete. Then on to Stockton. - the Railway Age was born.
10th October – The first regular passenger services began between Stockton and Darlington, the horse-drawn journey taking about 2 hours. Horses were retained for all passenger services and much of the freight work, as locomotive engines took some time to achieve reliability.

1826 - **26th January** – The first staithes were ready for use by the S&DR at Stockton. Coal cost 1/2d a ton.

1827 - Year ending 30.6.1827 – 18,588 tons shipped from Stockton.
Year ending 30.6.1828 – 52,900 tons shipped from Stockton.
The limitations of using Stockton included the River Tees itself and the size of ships built. Need for the S&DR to move downstream.
1st August – Serious damage was done along the wharves at Stockton when one of the locomotive engines of the S&DR was deliberately started

up and set off, causing much damage to both the locomotive and the wharves. A reward of 10 guineas was offered for conviction of the offenders.
19th October – Meeting about extending the S&DR downstream to Middlesbrough.
The *"Royal George"*, by Timothy Hackworth (The S&DR's Locomotive Superintendent), was the first reliable locomotive, with a capability of pulling 23 loaded coal wagons. This highly successful locomotive from the Hackworth range heralded the beginning of steam locomotion, finally taking over from horsepower.

1828 - The first ever locomotive railroad in America was built by the Stephensons (George and son Robert) for the Delaware and Hudson Canal Company.
19th January – Christopher Tennant has a letter printed in the "Durham County Advertiser" advocating his new railway company - the Clarence Railway Company.
March – Numerous meetings at Stockton, Darlington etc. either in favour of or against the projected railway.

Robert Stephenson (son of George)

23rd May – Royal Assent given to allow the Clarence Railway Company to run a line from Haverton Hill to Sim Pasture Farm, near Heighington in the County of Durham, connecting up to the S&DR line. It was further extended in 1829 and 1833 allowing alterations to the branch lines and extensions from Haverton Hill to Samphire Batts (Port Clarence) and from Samphire Batts to Saltholme.
23rd May – The S&DR gained Royal Assent for a branch from Stockton to Middlesbrough.
21st June – Christopher Tennant was the special guest of honour at a public dinner at Stockton, which also acknowledged the unstinting service of Henry Blanshard, held in honour of the Clarence Railway Company
July – The first General Meeting of the Clarence Railway Company.
August – Edward Pease's son, Joseph, was made responsible for the new S&DR development of Middlesbrough. Joseph Pease and 5 other Quaker gentlemen formed the "Owners of The Middlesbrough Estate". Land was purchased in May 1829 and the first house was built in April 1830.

1830 - **27th December** – Opening of the Middlesbrough branch of the S&DR

1831 - **1st January** – Opening of a new chain bridge across the River Tees at Stockton for the S&DR to pass through to Middlesbrough.

1832 - Norton Junction and the west curve were built as part of the Clarence Railway Company's system. This formed part of the Stockton Branch.

3rd April – A Bill to alter, amend, enlarge and extend the powers of several Acts passed in 1828 and 1829, for making and maintaining the Clarence Railway, received Royal Assent.

1st June – Royal Assent received for a Bill to establish a harbour and docks at Hartlepool, and for constructing a railway. In 1831, with Christopher Tennant's help, an Act was obtained to apply for Royal Assent.

1833 - **17th February** – A serious riot broke out between the Irish and English labourers on the Hartlepool railway line. The next week all the Irish labourers were driven out of the town. One was killed, another had his leg broken, and there were numerous injuries. A number of special constables were brought in to quell the riots.

29th March – Royal Assent obtained for the Clarence Railway Company to make a branch to Chilton.

May 11th - A case came before the magistrates in which Mr R Appleby of Wolviston and the Bishop of Durham sought from the Clarence Railway Company more compensation than had been offered, following a deviation of the plans originally proposed for the line at Haverton Hill. One company witness estimated the damage at £1,092, one of the claimant's witnesses at £8,800. The jury gave £3,500.

18th June – The Clarence Railway Bill for extending the line from Samphire Batts to Saltholme received Royal Assent.

August – By this time coals were being delivered to Stockton via the Stockton and Clarence branch lines.

September – Locomotive engines began to take over from horsepower on the S&DR lines. It was to be another 2 years before the Clarence Railway began introducing steam on some lines.

29th October – The Clarence Railway Company's own staithes were in use at Stockton Quayside.

Fossick's Bridge ("Fuzzy" Bridge) was erected to carry the Clarence Railway line across Darlington Lane on its approach to Norton Junction.

1834 - **30th January** – A small staith at Haverton Hill was opened up, followed a few months later by a deep water staith at Samphire Batts (Port Clarence). In 1839 over a quarter of a million tons of coal were shipped from these staithes.

1835 - **11th July** – The first coaches ran on the Clarence Railway Company's lines between Stockton and Durham.
Around this time the Clarence Railway Company put up the Norton Road (North Shore) Junction Station for its passengers.

1836 - **17th February** – A tremendous hurricane from the north-east caused the River Tees to rise higher than previously known, even washing away part of the railway between Stockton and Middlesbrough.

1837 - During this year an Act was passed for making a railway to connect up the Great North, the Hartlepool and Clarence railways.
21st July - 3 men and a boy lost their lives in a fire on a ship called *"The James"* of Perth, whilst berthed at the Clarence staithes in Stockton.

1838 - **12th September** – Christopher Tennant (the founder of the Clarence Railway Company) died suddenly this day. He was buried at in the graveyard of St Hilda's church, Hartlepool.

1839 - **19th March** – Near Bishop Middleham, an engine and 2 coaches ran off the Clarence Railway. The engine dragged one of the coaches halfway down an embankment after it, when a coupling chain broke. The engineman, fireman and guard were all killed. No passengers were hurt.

1839/40 George Fossick of Clapham and Thomas Hackworth of Shildon took over a flour and saw mill (previously in the occupation of Mr Jacob Waller) situated on Norton Road near Stockton. From these premises they established a much-respected locomotive engine manufactory which supplied engines and wagons initially for the Clarence Railway Company and then to the Hartlepool and other railway companies. Thomas Hackworth was a brother of Timothy Hackworth of Shildon, (who had become the first Locomotive Superintendent of the Stockton & Darlington Railway Company, at George Stephenson's request). "Fuzzy" bridge, between The Glebe and Ragworth/Blue Hall estates is named after George Fossick.

1840 - **12th November** – Coal was carried for the first time on the Stockton and Hartlepool Railway. Passenger and general merchandise traffic began on **10th February 1841**.
The S&DR had commenced a line to Hartlepool by a junction with the Clarence Railway branch near Billingham.

1841 - **4th January** – The Great North of England Railway began carrying coals and merchandise. This meant that goods carried into Stockton could be taken by train to Darlington and then on to York. From **31st March** passengers could travel from Norton Junction to Darlington and change to go to York.

10th February – The Stockton to Hartlepool Railway had been opened officially the day before. Today it was open for public use. The viaduct of this railway at Greatham has 92 arches and is about _ a mile long.

7th April- The delivery of mail posted from London the evening before now reached its local destination by 2 p.m. on the following day, due to the Great North of England Railway having been completed, thus forming a direct link to the metropolis.

9th June – Fossick & Hackworth's Steam Engine Manufactory on Norton Road delivered the earliest of the Stockton & Darlington Railway Company's locomotive engine – called ***"The Stockton"***.

Development of the Norton Junction "triangle" began to take place during the leasing of the line by the Stockton & Hartlepool Railway Company, when a new curve to the east of the line in use made travelling to Hartlepool much easier.

1842 - **15th November** – The first coals from Brancepeth Park colliery were sent via West Durham and the Clarence Railway for shipment from Stockton.

Some time this year a new passenger station was built on Norton Road for the Hartlepool & Stockton Railway Company, adjoining one built in 1835 for the Clarence Railway Company.

1843 - **November**- A coach train crash took place on the Clarence Railway curve line near Billingham Station. Miraculously, no-one was hurt, although damage to the coaches, engines and (empty) wagons was estimated at more than £300.

1844 - In this year Mr Thomas Hutchinson, an eminent railway contractor, was killed near Sedgefield by a train of wagons on the Clarence Railway.

27th May – The first train of wagons passed over the Stockton & Darlington Company's new iron bridge at Stockton. It had been built to replace the 274 ft. long suspension bridge built by Capt. Brown, R.N. in 1830, the bridge having been judged to be incapable of taking the increased traffic.

18th June – It was now possible, since the linking up of the Newcastle & Darlington Junction Railway, to travel from Newcastle to London by railway train with only one change at Darlington. It took passengers only 8 hours, mail took $9^1/_2$ hours. The last mail coaches ran on this day, with the odd exception. (The first mail coaches from London to Newcastle had begun running in 1786, taking 45 hours – now it took only one-fifth of the time.)

August – Around this time the Clarence Railway, which had so far proved unprofitable and had been offered for sale by the Public Works Loans Commissioner, was leased for 21 years by the Stockton & Hartlepool Railway Company.

1845 - **26th July** – Leonard Raisbeck died at Stockton aged 67. He had been a solicitor and a Commissioner of the Peace. He had been Mayor of Stockton in 1832, Stockton's Recorder for a time, Steward of the Bishop's Court at Stockton (1804-1826) and Commander of the Stockton Volunteers. He had held numerous offices throughout his life and was much respected. He had been presented in 1845 with an epergne bearing the arms of the Corporation of Stockton and his own arms – a testimony to the high esteem in which he was held. He had been instrumental in pushing forward the Stockton & Darlington Railway Company after the Stockton to Auckland Canal Scheme fell through in 1818. In 1828 he was in opposition, and resigned as Chairman of the Company when there were plans to make Middlesbrough the next new port and town to be connected to the S&DR, he believed, in detriment to Stockton.

1846 - **21st May** – The Stockton & Darlington Railway Company opened a new station at Stockton.

Prime Minister Robert Peel's Railway Passenger (Cheap Trains) Act was brought in this year. This stated that every railway company had to run at least one train every day on every line on which they had to carry passengers at only 1d per mile.

1848 - **5th April** – Messrs Fossick & Hackworth's Locomotive Engine Building establishment on Norton Road suffered a disastrous fire, in which a large number of valuable patterns and joiners' and smiths' tools were destroyed.

19th September – The Stockton & Darlington Railway station house at Stockton was the venue for 2 days of a bazaar organised by Lady Londonderry. The proceeds were to be spent on a new church at Thorpe Thewles.

1849 - **28th September**- A number of special trains left today from Hartlepool, Norton and Stockton taking hundreds of people to Darlington to see Her Majesty Queen Victoria (who had consented to have her train halted on the way to Scotland) in order to receive a loyal address from the inhabitants of Darlington at Bank Top Station. For the Darlington residents the day was declared a holiday and Bank Top Station was hung with flags and bunting and a triumphal arch.
A viaduct was begun across the River Tees, running through Yarm (opened in 1852).

1850 - **7th July**- Timothy Hackworth of Shildon, locomotive engine designer, died aged 66. He was the brother of Thomas Hackworth of Fossick & Hackworth fame, Norton Road near Stockton.

1851 - **7th January** – The Stockton & Hartlepool Railway Company leased the line in perpetuity from the Clarence Railway Company at $2^1/_2$% on the share capital, the lessees paying off the government and other debts. In 1852 a Bill was passed to amalgamate under the Hartlepool Railway banner.

1852 - **15th May** – Yarm viaduct was opened to traffic. It had been built by contractors Messrs James Trowsdale & Co. for the Leeds Northern Railway (formerly the Thirsk & Leeds Railway Company) to connect Thirsk with Stockton and Hartlepool. It spanned the River Tees from the County Durham side near Eaglescliffe to the Yorkshire side along the back of Yarm's high street. It was 760 yards long, with 43 arches, using $7^1/_2$ million bricks and 139,000 cu.ft. of stone, at a cost of £44,500. (Yarm had been the birthplace and pioneer of the railways).
2nd June – The new station was opened on Bishopton Road by the Leeds Northern Railway Company, necessitated by the increased amount of rail traffic which had travelled since the Great Exhibition in London a year earlier.
30th June – The amalgamation of the SH&CR Company and the Clarence Railway Company and the Hartlepool Harbour and Dock Company received Royal Assent.

21st July – A fatal collision took place at Norton between a passenger train from Ferryhill and a Leeds Northern luggage train. 2 of the carriages were shattered, during which Mr Grainger, an engineer from Edinburgh, had both legs broken, and died a few days later of his injuries. 2 ladies were injured in like manner, one of them also dying a day or two later. Other people were injured too. The driver was tried for manslaughter at the Durham Assizes and served a sentence of imprisonment.

This year the West Hartlepool Harbour and Railway Company came into being under Ralph Ward Jackson after the amalgamation of the Clarence Railway Company, the Stockton and Hartlepool Railway Company and the Hartlepool West Harbour and Dock Company.

1853 – Fossick & Hackworth's Locomotive Engine Manufactory on Norton Road had progressed to making marine engines and this year saw the first pair of marine engines produced under the management of Mr Robert Thorman.

1856 - **6th August** – Norton's claim to fame came with the casting of one of the "Big Ben" bells at the ironworks of Warner, Lucas & Barrett, situated down Cross-Dike Lane (Station Road). It had been transported to Hartlepool Docks from Norton Station and then on to London.

1858 - **30th June** - The local railway returns recorded that the West Hartlepool Railway Company employed 890 people, among them 73 engine drivers, 72 firemen, 42 labourers and 38 unspecified (mainly in the coal trade through Norton to Hartlepool).

1859 - **31st May** - An alarming incident occurred on the railway line near Preston (near Stockton) caused by a loose rail being left by the platelayers. The express from Middlesbrough to Darlington left Stockton at half-past-one and on arriving at the spot struck the rail and was thrown off the line. 5 carriages were embedded on the edge of an embankment while the last 3 carriages toppled over the embankment. Many passengers were slightly bruised and one female passenger received internal injuries.

1863 - **July** – One of the Acts passed during the parliamentary session enabled the Stockton & Darlington Railway Company to merge

with the North Eastern Railway Company.

4th November – The clearing house at the Stockton station of the West Hartlepool Railway was so badly damaged that everything in it was moved or broken after a goods train ran into it and moved it.

1864 - **25th October**- 11 wagons on the S&DR, near the goods station at Stockton, were smashed to pieces in an accident. A similar incident occurred the next day on the same line at Preston Junction. Messrs Fossick & Hackworth, situated on Norton Road, became known this year as Fossick, Blair & Co. Ltd. They principally built marine engines under the direction of George Blair, on a 23-acre site, employing 1,600 men. Their reputation was world-wide, and they had fitting out shops and wharves at the riverside.

1865 - **4th April** - A mail train bound for Middlesbrough ran into 6 laden coal wagons which had been left on the line near Hartburn cutting. The wagons were demolished, with debris spread over a 50 yard area. One or two of the first-class passengers received slight facial bruising.

On this same day a horse driver at the Stockton Malleable Iron Works on Norton Road received injuries when he got jammed between the buffers of 2 wagons and was taken to the Surgical Hospital. He died within 3 hours of the accident.

20th May – The bridge over the railway, near the top of Paradise Street in Stockton, was to be removed with the object of making a sub-way in its place.
30th June – The West Hartlepool Harbour and Railway Company merged with the North Eastern Railway Company.
1st August- From this day the line running from Spennymoor and Coxhoe to Port Clarence and the Hartlepools is to be known as "The West Hartlepool Section of the North Eastern Railway".
16th October – A collision took place between a passenger train and a wagon train on the railway near Port Clarence, when the signals were not altered. The passengers were thrown from their seats but were not badly hurt.

1866 - George Fossick of Fossick & Hackworth on Norton Road died this year.

1875 - The Queens Hotel, situated near the North Stockton Railway Station, was built this year to accommodate the immense passenger traffic using the railway station. It was built on 3 storeys, with 40 private and public rooms and lots of scope for extension when the new station, then still in the course of being built, was completed. (The building was destroyed by a fire in the early 1980s).

1877 - Thorpe Thewles viaduct was completed this year, having been started in 1875, to carry the Stockton & Castle Eden Branch Railway across the Thorpe Beck. It was 461 yards long and had 21 arches. (It was demolished on 3rd June 1979).
The NER opened the first stretch of the Bowesfield-Wellfield line.

1879 - Norton's Iron Works closed down, helped along by a disastrous strike which crippled the whole iron industry in the area in 1866. The houses which had been built for the Iron Works in 1855 were sold to the North Eastern Railway Company and remained empty until 1899 when the Stone & Concrete Works opened, and their workers lived in the houses. The children attended Norton Board School and were known locally as "The Furnace Children", although their correct address was in fact Station Road (then leading to Calf Fallow Lane). A new estate of private houses now occupies the site – Forest Park.

1880 - 1st March – The North-Eastern Railway Company opened a line from Bowesfield Junction at Stockton.

1886 - 2nd March – A blizzard buried a train travelling from Seaham on the Londonderry line in snowdrifts south of Ryhope. 6 carriages with 4 engines (2 to pull and 2 to push) were dug out by the following afternoon when hundreds of men cleared the blocked lines, having begun to dig them out from 4 a.m. The snowstorm lasted 4 days and it was the worst in north-east railway history to that date.

1889 - Small-gauge stone railway sleepers laid to a gravel pit in Hawes Wood (near Harper's Garden Centre) to carry gravel to the Stockton Stone & Concrete Works in Station Road, Norton.

1948 - The Junction Chapel closed and a new one was built at Ragworth.

1963 - The year the Beeching "axe" closed a number of rural railway stations.

1981 - Several of the original railway buildings at Norton Junction were demolished.

Sources of Information

Census Forms for 1841, 1851, 1861, 1871 and 1881
Wards Directory for 1851
Tomlinson W.W. The North Eastern Railway –
Its Rise and Development,1914
Semmens P.W.B. Exploring the Stockton and Darlington Railway, 1975
Holmes P.J. Stockton and Darlington Railway, 1825-1975
McDougall C.A. The Stockton and Darlington Railway, 1821-18652
(Local History Publication No.9), 1975
Hoole K. Railways of Teesside, 1982
Moorsom N. Stockton and Darlington Railway, The Foundation of
Middlesbrough, 1975
Sowler T.H. A History of The Town and Borough of Stockton, 1972
North G.A. Teesside's Economic Heritage
Brewster J. History of Stockton upon Tees, 1829
Richmond T. The Local Records of Stockton and the Neighbourhood, 1868
Railway Centenary Committee. The Railway Centenary 1825-1925,
Stockton upon Tees
Heavisides H. The Annals of Stockton-on-Tees, 1865
Finch R. Coals From Newcastle, 1973

Thorpe Thewles Viaduct

Whilst every effort has been made to contact the original owners of pictures, we apologise to anyone who may have inadvertently been omitted from the acknowledgements.

Acknowledgements

We are eternally grateful to the following:

Mike Burton for the illustrations (front page and pages 31, 33 and 54)
Mrs Glass for information and illustration on page 31
Mr Gadsby for providing help with the maps
Tom Sowler for personal information
David Summerfield for help with pages 39-47
Gretta Percy for sketch of Blackroods Farm on page 49
Charles Harland Thompson for the poem "Farmer's Lament"
Steven Cook and staff at Realise I.T., Billingham, for help and patience
June McConnell and Patricia Youdale for invaluable help and support
The staff at Stockton Reference Library for information and assistance
Mandy Fearns for help with editing and compilation
Mr and Mrs G Fell of Norton for information and photographs, page 32
Ivan Harrington, for invaluable help in providing, developing and printing all other photographs, selected from his fantastic collection

Bob Harbron of Norton Heritage -
Norton Heritage, under the able leadership of the inexhaustible Bob Harbron, continues to conduct "Walks and Talks" around Norton and the surrounding districts, as well as issuing leaflets on all aspects of its history, and is always happy to offer help of an historical nature. Norton Heritage can be contacted at 83 Leven Road, Norton, Stockton on Tees, TS20 1DB (01642) 559747

Norton Station

About the Author

Well-known local historian Carol Fox is the mother of 2 grown-up children, and Nanna to 2 lively young grandsons, Garrin and Dillon. Besides working as a Medical Secretary at the local General Hospital in Stockton, she is kept very busy with her diverse hobbies and interests. As well as writing, she spends much of her time involved with dolls houses and miniatures, and is an avid Star Trek fan. She is the younger sister of Patricia and twin sister of June, without whose help this book could not have been published.

Carol has also been encouraged in this project by Bob Harbron of Norton Heritage. "*The Iron Road*" was initially inspired back in 1981 when a number of original buildings were demolished at Norton Junction. At that time, Carol wrote a booklet in conjunction with Norton Heritage Group depicting Norton Junction and the Clarence Railway. The popularity of the booklet over the last 2 decades has encouraged people to submit further information and new photographs. As a result, this has prompted Carol to rewrite the booklet and so bring it up-to-date for the 21st Century. Ever keen to bring local history into schools and educational institutions, Carol presents "*An Illustrated History of Norton: The Iron Road*" as the first in a series of books bringing Norton's past to life.

Published by Fearns & Co., 6 Cheviot Crescent, Billingham TS23 2PS
Printed by Billingham Press

ISBN 1 903678 00 5